Opinions About

ODYSSEUS:
A GREEK HERO

by Cynthia Swain • illustrated by Jose Ramos

D0028040

TABLE OF CONTENTS

INTRODUCTION

THE ODYSSEY:
One Man's Journey Home from War

Myths and legends are exciting tales about gods, heroes, and monsters. The ancient Greeks had many myths and legends. About 2,800 years ago, a man named Homer decided to write down some of these tales. He called one of his books *The Odyssey*.

In *The Odyssey*, a king named Odysseus goes off to war with his men. For ten long years, they fight many terrible battles. After the war is won, Odysseus and his men long to return to their home, the Greek island of Ithaca.

They set sail for their beloved island, but they encounter many challenges along the way. They get lost. They experience terrible storms. Monsters try to kill them. None of King Odysseus's men survive the journey, but Odysseus is very crafty, and after twenty long years away from home, he finally returns to Ithaca to be reunited with his wife and son.

Read two famous scenes from *The Odyssey* to learn more about the famous character Odysseus.

THE
ODYSSEY

ODYSSEUS

Fools the Cyclops

One day Odysseus and his men spotted an island in the distance. Odysseus ordered his men to dock the ship.

"We must search this land for supplies or we will starve," the leader said. His men brought the boat onto land to begin their search.

"What do you know of this island?" Odysseus asked his men. He did not recall ever seeing this land during his previous journeys. "Does it have animals we can hunt? Is there a river where we can find clean water?"

None of his men knew the island either. So they decided to climb to the top of the hill for a clear view. When they arrived, they looked all around. They could see that the island was filled with mountains and large trees. There were no homes or farms. It was a wild place.

"We must be careful here," said Odysseus. "Let us find what we need and quickly leave this island. I do not like this place."

"Tell us what we should do, my king," said Odysseus's most trusted man.

"I need you to be our scout and warn us of what lies ahead," the king said. "Take this spear in case you run into trouble." So the scout set off on his mission.

An hour later, Odysseus and his men heard the scout calling them, and they ran as fast as they could up a mountain path. When they reached the scout, they could not believe their eyes—it was the answer to all their needs.

"Look at all these sheep," the scout said proudly. There were many animals grazing on the mountainside.

Odysseus was very pleased, but he was also puzzled. "Where are they going?"

"They are entering that **deserted** cave." He pointed. "They are seeking shelter for the evening."

"We must trap them all in the cave so we can kill as many as possible," the king said.

"I would not do that, my king," the scout warned.

"Why not?" Odysseus barked his reply. He was not used to having one of his men question his decision.

"The cave is dark. We don't know what is inside," the scout explained. "Why not just lead the sheep outside the cave to our ship and leave this dreadful island?"

"Never doubt my judgment," Odysseus shouted at his trusted scout. "Do as I say!"

So the king's men did as they were told and surrounded the sheep. They led them into the dark cave. One of the men lit a torch, and they all marveled at how many sheep they had.

Suddenly, they heard a terrible **din**. They turned around and saw that the cave entrance was now blocked by a huge boulder. In front of that stone was a **ferocious** giant. They were trapped.

"I am Cyclops. How dare you enter my cave and try to steal my sheep! You are now my prisoners and I will kill you all!" Cyclops was from a race of violent giants that lived on the island. He had only one huge eye in the middle of his forehead.

The giant raced toward the men. With his enormous hands, he grabbed a few of them and swallowed them up. The other men ran to the side of the cave and begged for their lives.

7

But Odysseus did not run or beg. He stayed calm and waited for a moment. Then he bravely walked up to Cyclops and spoke to him. "Please accept my apology, Cyclops. I did not know that this was your home. I had no idea that you owned these sheep."

Cyclops snarled at Odysseus.

"To show you how sorry I am, please share my precious wine." Odysseus took his wineskin and offered it to Cyclops. "Please, help yourself."

The giant was thirsty, so he took a long drink.

"Have as much as you want." Odysseus encouraged the giant to keep drinking.

"I accept your apology. Thank you for your **hospitality**." The giant took another long drink. "What is your name?"

The crafty king of Ithaca smiled. "My name is . . . No One."

"Thank you, No One." The giant kept drinking. Eventually he drank so much wine that he fell asleep on the floor of the cave.

Then Odysseus gathered up his men and whispered to them. "Everyone go and find a sheep and hide beneath it. Do not come out until I give the order."

"Hide? Why?" asked one of the puzzled men. "We should be trying to escape!"

"Just do as I say," commanded Odysseus. The men did not understand, but they did as they were told. Then Odysseus took back the sharp spear that he had given to the scout. The king slowly crept near the head of the snoring Cyclops. With all his strength, he rammed the stick deeply into the eye of the giant and ran to hide under a large sheep.

The giant howled in pain. "What have you done to me? Where are you, No One? I cannot see! I am blind!" In agony, Cyclops leapt to his feet.

When the other giants heard the screaming, they ran to the cave. They rolled the boulder away, leaned in, and shouted. "Who is hurting you, our brother?"

Cyclops moaned, "No One! No One is hurting me!"

"No one? That's ridiculous," the brothers laughed. They thought their brother was joking with them. How could the giant be in any trouble, when no one was bothering him? The brothers turned away and left to tend their own sheep.

Cyclops was furious now. "You will pay for what you have done to me," the giant shouted to Odysseus and his men.

Cyclops could not see where the men were hiding, so he used his hands to feel around the cave. Each time he tried, he could not find the men. All he could feel was the woolly backs of his sheep. He cried out in frustration. "Where is No One?!"

Silently, Odysseus signaled for his men to cling tightly to the sheep as they walked out of the cave. Once they were free, the men ran to the ship and escaped the island.

ODYSSEUS
and the Suitors

After twenty years, Odysseus finally stepped onto the shores of Ithaca. He longed to be king again and find his faithful wife Penelope and son Telemachus.

But first the goddess Athena came to him. "Listen carefully, Odysseus. There is danger here. You must go to the castle in **disguise**. A hundred or more evil men have come to Ithaca. They told your wife that you are dead and that she should marry one of them. They don't care about her. They just want to be king. They have taken over your household. They drink your wine and eat your food. They will not go unless you drive them out."

Odysseus grew angry, but he followed Athena's advice and disguised himself. When he arrived at the castle dressed as a beggar, Odysseus saw Penelope and Telemachus and secretly called them over.

"I am Odysseus, your husband, your father, and your king," he whispered to them.

"No, that cannot be," exclaimed Penelope. "My husband is dead. You are a mere beggar! You are pretending to be the king."

"Look into my eyes," Odysseus said. "Don't you know me? Can't you see that I am your rightful king?"

Penelope and Telemachus looked closely at the beggar. They immediately recognized him. Odysseus was indeed their king.

"Let us **proclaim** to the court that the king is not dead," said Penelope, who was overjoyed to see her husband.

"Hush," warned Odysseus. "The **suitors** will kill us all if they find out who I am. Wait. I have a plan to fool them and take back the kingdom." The king revealed his plan to his wife and son and they agreed to do their part.

"Father, I will do as you say and hide the weapons of the suitors," Telemachus said.

"Husband, I will announce to all in the court that there will be a contest to decide who will marry me and become king."

So Penelope walked to her throne and called everyone to attention, while Telemachus gathered all the weapons and hid them. "Whoever is able to string Odysseus's bow and shoot an arrow through twelve ax handles will win my hand and become king of Ithaca," Penelope announced to the gathered suitors.

Each suitor tried and failed. Only one person had the skill and the strength to do that. It was the beggar.

"I am Odysseus, king of Ithaca!" He threw off his disguise and grabbed a sword. "You must all die for trying to steal my crown and harming my family and my kingdom."

The evil suitors were shocked and began looking for their weapons. But they were missing. Then Odysseus, the goddess Athena, and his son Telemachus together killed every suitor.

Once again, Odysseus could take his rightful place as king. But Odysseus still lived in fear. He was afraid that the families of the suitors would try to **avenge** their deaths.

READ AND EVALUATE OPINIONS ABOUT ODYSSEUS

Now that you've read episodes from the classic book *The Odyssey*, let's read three writers' opinions about Odysseus's actions in these episodes. Each writer was given the same writing prompt, shown below. The writers each have a different opinion, yet each provides a good example of writing a strong argument. A well-written opinion is backed up by reasons, uses transition words, and has a concluding statement. In the first opinion piece, annotations have been added to help you identify these important parts of an opinion piece.

Opinion Writing Prompt:

Think about the two episodes from *The Odyssey* that you read. In the first episode, Odysseus blinded Cyclops. In the second episode, he killed the suitors in his castle. Did he need to use violence, or could he have found a less violent solution? State your opinion and defend it **using evidence from the text.**

OPINION 1

Odysseus Has No Choice!

The writer begins with a clearly stated opinion.

The writer creates an organizational structure that lists reasons for the opinion.

Odysseus has no choice but to blind Cyclops and kill the suitors. <u>In both</u> episodes, he faces a life-or-death situation. His actions are necessary. They are justified, too, <u>because</u> he has done nothing wrong yet his enemies all want to kill him and his men.

The writer uses linking words to connect opinions and reasons.

The writer uses evidence from the text to support the first reason.

The writer continues to use linking words to connect opinions and reasons.

In "Odysseus Fools the Cyclops," the one-eyed evil monster shows no sympathy. "You are now my prisoners, and I will kill you all!" he says. <u>Then</u> he picks up several men and eats them. This monster would never show mercy. Odysseus has to blind the monster <u>or</u> he and his men will not escape.

In "Odysseus and the Suitors," Athena warns Odysseus that he is in danger. "A hundred or more evil men have come to Ithaca," she says. His enemies outnumber him. He knows they will stop at nothing. They want to take his throne. They want to marry his wife. They are going to stop at nothing to kill him. If they got away, they might return with an army. He has to slay them.

> The writer uses evidence from the text to support the first reason.

In both episodes from *The Odyssey*, Odysseus faces terrible situations. As a result, he has no choice but to kill his enemies. He is innocent of wrongdoings.

> The writer provides a concluding statement or section.

Odysseus Makes the Wrong Choices

Odysseus should not blind Cyclops, nor should he kill all the suitors. He is known to be a crafty leader. He has lots of tricks up his sleeve. He should at least try to find nonviolent ways to solve his problems. Violence should always be the last resort.

In "Odysseus Fools the Cyclops," there is no justification for blinding the giant. Odysseus's clever plan to stop the giant from eating more men is already working. By sharing his wine, the king calms Cyclops down and the giant becomes friendly. As a result, the giant says, "Thank you for your hospitality." Odysseus should continue to be friendly. Furthermore, he could offer the giant even more gifts and bargain for his men's safety. But he doesn't even try a peaceful solution.

In "Odysseus and the Suitors," there is no reason for Odysseus to kill all the suitors. They are certainly terrible guests, but they have done no real harm. Instead of killing them all, Odysseus could hide their weapons and then just tell them all to leave or else. Without their weapons, these suitors would probably run away. But Odysseus gives them no choice. He slaughters them. Given his situation, there is no excuse for so much unnecessary bloodshed.

Odysseus is a very smart leader who does not have to resort to violence. He is clever enough to make a friend of Cyclops and scare away the suitors. Instead, he lets his anger get the better of him and uses violence to solve his problems. To summarize, violence is always the wrong first choice.

One Smart Choice, One Poor Choice

The king makes one smart choice and one absolutely foolish choice! In "Odysseus Fools the Cyclops," the king makes a smart choice because the cyclops monster is going to kill him and his men. Cyclops has to be stopped! But in the story "Odysseus and the Suitors," the king doesn't just stop the suitors. Instead, he kills them! He is not thinking ahead. As a result, his poor choice leads people to be killed unnecessarily.

In the first story, Cyclops obviously has no intention of letting the king and his men go. That is why the giant has closed the entrance to the cave with a boulder. The only way they can escape is to weaken the giant. In fact, the king could do something even more violent and kill Cyclops! Yet the king spares the giant's life.

In the second story, Odysseus does not think ahead when he kills the suitors. He should be asking himself: *What will happen if I kill them all?* Instead, he waits until all the suitors are dead to consider that. The story says: "But Odysseus still lived in fear. He was afraid that the families of the suitors would try to avenge their deaths." Consequently, killing can lead to even more killing—and fear of being killed.

Despite threats of violence, people should respond with violence only when absolutely necessary. When the king and his men are trapped and have no other way out, Odysseus is justified in blinding the giant to stop him. Odysseus, as king, has to protect his men. But in dealing with the suitors, Odysseus has other options that he isn't even trying. And as mentioned earlier, many people suffer the consequences of that violence. And Odysseus lives thereafter in fear of revenge.

EVALUATE THE OPINION TEXTS

Reread each opinion piece, and evaluate it using the rubric below as a guide. Write your evaluation of each piece on a separate piece of paper. Do the writers include the important elements?

Opinion Writing Rubric				
Opinion Traits	1	2	3	4
The writer states a strong opinion, position, or point of view.				
The writer supplies well-organized reasons that support his or her opinion using facts, concrete examples, and supporting evidence from the text.				
The writer links opinions and reasons using words, phrases, and clauses.				
The writer provides a concluding statement or section that supports the position.				

GLOSSARY

avenge	(uh-VENJ) *verb* to harm someone to punish him or her for a bad deed (page 14)
deserted	(dih-ZER-ted) *adjective* having no people living there at that time (page 6)
din	(DIN) *noun* a loud, continuous noise (page 7)
disguise	(dih-SKIZE) *noun* a deliberate change in appearance to avoid being recognized (page 12)
ferocious	(fuh-ROH-shes) *adjective* very mean, cruel, fierce (page 7)
hospitality	(hahs-pih-TA-lih-tee) *noun* friendly and generous treatment of guests or strangers (page 9)
proclaim	(proh-KLAME) *verb* to declare publicly; to make an announcement (page 13)
suitors	(SOO-terz) *noun* men who seek to date and marry women (page 13)

ANALYZE THE TEXT

Questions for Close Reading

Use facts and details from the text to support your answers to the following questions.

- Reread pages 8–9. What happens after Odysseus encourages the giant to keep drinking the wine? Why is this detail important to the story?

- On page 9, Odysseus's men do not want to follow his order. They want to run. What would you have done?

- Reread the first two paragraphs on page 12. What do they tell you about the relationship between Odysseus and Athena?

- Even problems that appear to be impossible have solutions. What evidence from the two stories supports this theme?

Comprehension: Character Analysis

Odysseus has a strong will and wants things done his way. He is also patient when he needs to be. Cite details from both stories that prove Odysseus has these character traits.

Strong willed	Patient